3-10

DATE DUE

Reading Essentials
in Social Studies

U.S. NATIONAL PARKS TOUR

Carlsbad Caverns

SARA LOUISE KRAS

Perfection Learning®

EDITORIAL DIRECTOR	Susan C. Thies
EDITOR	Mary L. Bush
COVER DESIGN	Mike Aspengren
INSIDE DESIGN	Mark Hagenberg
PHOTO RESEARCH	Lisa Lorimor

Acknowledgments

Many thanks to Robert Hoff, Carlsbad Caverns Historian, for taking my husband and me through the park and for sharing all the historical stories and current facts about the cave.

Also thanks to Myra Barnes, Carlsbad Caverns Wildlife Biologist, for answering my many questions about bats and other wildlife in the Carlsbad area.

And thanks to Paul Burger, Carlsbad Caverns Hydrologist, for patiently explaining how a cave is formed.

To my brothers Paul and Keith Jarvis, my first companions to Carlsbad Caverns

IMAGE CREDITS

Bat Conservation International: pp. 23, 24, 37 (top); Joe Kras: cover (bottom images), pp. 4–5, 7, 8–9, 11, 12, 13 (top), 14, 15 (top), 16, 20, 21, 25, 26 (top), 27 (bottom), 28, 29, 30, 31 (bottom), 32, 33, 34, 35, 36–37, 38

ArtToday: pp. 31 (top), 36 (top); Corel: cover (full page), pp. 1, 3, 6, 9 (right), 10, 22, 26–27, 39, 40; National Park Service: pp. 13 (right), 17, 18, 19; Photodisc: p. 15 (center)

Perfection Learning® Corporation
1000 North Second Avenue, P.O. Box 500
Logan, Iowa 51546-0500.
Phone: 1-800-831-4190
Fax: 1-800-543-2745
perfectionlearning.com

1 2 3 4 5 BA 06 05 04 03 02

ISBN 0-7891-5843-4

Contents

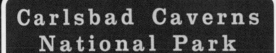

Carlsbad Caverns National Park

Elevation Above Sea Level:

Here 4408
Plains Below 3600
Cavern Floor Beneath 3652

NATIONAL PARK SERVICE
Department of the Interior

Introduction to
Carlsbad Caverns

A sidewalk leads down to the natural entrance of the cavern. Along the walk are desert plants and shrubs. All of a sudden, the ground opens wide. At the end of the huge hole is complete darkness. A **switchback** path takes you deeper and deeper into the darkness. You have now entered the magical world of Carlsbad Cavern.

Singular or Plural?

Carlsbad Caverns refers to the area known as Carlsbad Caverns National Park, which includes more than 80 caves, or caverns. Carlsbad Cavern is just one of these caves—however, it is the one that is most developed for tourist exploration.

Guadalupe Mountains, but none of the others are as famous as Carlsbad Caverns.

Carlsbad Becomes a National Park

President Calvin Coolidge established Carlsbad Cavern as a national monument in 1923. Then in 1930, President Herbert Hoover signed a bill making Carlsbad Caverns a national park. On December 6, 1995, Carlsbad became a World Heritage Site as well.

What's a World Heritage Site?

World Heritage Sites are cultural and natural places that are considered important to the world. Once a building or natural landform becomes a World Heritage Site, it is preserved and protected from damage. Other U.S. National Parks that are also World Heritage Sites include Yosemite, Yellowstone, Grand Canyon, Redwood, and Everglades.

Carlsbad Caverns National Park contains over 80 caves, or caverns. Carlsbad Cavern is one of the largest of these caves. It has huge underground chambers and endless natural formations.

The park is in southeast New Mexico. It is part of the Chihuahuan Desert, located in the Guadalupe Mountains. Many caves have been discovered in the

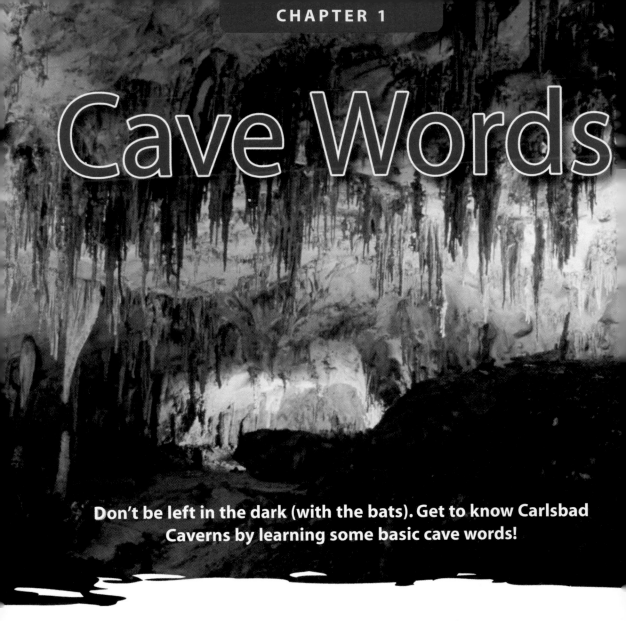

CHAPTER 1

Cave Words

Don't be left in the dark (with the bats). Get to know Carlsbad Caverns by learning some basic cave words!

calcite

Calcite is a mineral formed from limestone and other minerals. It is found in the water that drips or seeps into caves. When the water **evaporates**, the calcite is left behind. Most cave formations are made of calcite.

cave formation

A cave formation is a **deposit** of calcite found in caves. Straws, stalactites, stalagmites, columns, draperies, popcorn or cave coral, and flowstone are all cave formations.

cavern

A cavern, or cave, is a huge open space under the ground.

column

When a stalactite and a stalagmite grow together, it is called a *column*. A column stretches from the floor of the cave all the way up to the ceiling.

drapery

A drapery is a wide, thin, flat stalactite. It looks like a long curtain, or drapery. Some draperies extend from a cave's ceiling to its floor.

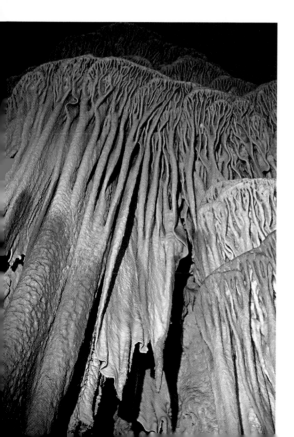

Scientifically Speaking

The scientific term for a cave formation is *speleothem*. Speleothems are the natural mineral formations or deposits occurring in a cave, such as stalagmites, stalactites, and soda straws.

flowstone

When water flows over the walls and floors of a cave, layers of calcite build up. These layers are called *flowstone*.

gypsum

Gypsum is a mineral formed when limestone is dissolved by sulfuric acid. Gypsum deposits are **sediments** from ancient inland seas and are often found on the floors of caves.

limestone

Limestone is a soft rock formed from the remains of living things. It is easily shaped and dissolved by acids. Most caves have walls of limestone.

Drapery formations got their name from the ripples and folds caused by water flow and the multicolored bands that appear from the presence of different minerals.

popcorn or cave coral

Popcorn, also called *cave coral*, forms on the walls of a cave when water evaporates, leaving calcite crystals behind. The crystals grow in small clusters that look like popcorn and have a rough texture.

soda straw

A soda straw is a thin, hollow tube of calcite hanging from a cave's ceiling. Water drips through the straw's center, leaving calcite behind. When the center of a hollow straw becomes plugged, it often turns into a stalactite.

speleologist

A speleologist is a scientist who explores caves. Speleologists are experts on how caves are made and the animals that live in caves. They make maps of caves and record formations and other cave discoveries.

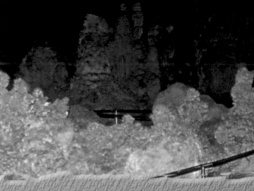

Huge stalagmites grow along the sidewalk path through the Big Room of Carlsbad Cavern.

Ground or Ceiling?

If you're having trouble remembering the difference between a stalactite and a stalagmite, use these hints.

Stala**c**tites grow from the **c**eiling, while stala**g**mites grow from the **g**round.

Stala**ctites** hold **tight** to the ceiling. Stalag**mites might** reach the ceiling someday.

What's the Deal with "Spel"?

The "spel" in *speleothem*, *speleologist*, and *spelunker* comes from the Latin word *speleum* and the Greek word *spelaion*, which mean "cave."

spelunker

A spelunker is a person who explores caves for fun. Beginning spelunkers can tour caves that are open to the public like Carlsbad Cavern. Experienced spelunkers sometimes explore wild caves, or caves that have not been developed or opened for tourism.

stalactite

A stalactite is a calcite formation that looks like an icicle hanging from the ceiling of a cave. As the water dripping from a cave's ceiling evaporates, the calcite hardens into a pointed stalactite. These formations are created over millions of years—one drip of water at a time.

stalagmite

Stalagmites look like cones growing up from the ground. When dripping water reaches the floor of a cave, the calcite in the water hardens and builds a stalagmite.

sulfuric acid

When the oxygen in water combines with the gas hydrogen sulfide, sulfuric acid is created. This is a very strong acid that dissolves or burns many substances.

stalactites

stalagmites

CHAPTER 2

How Were the Caves Formed?

Caves usually form in mountain areas with a lot of moisture. The caverns of Carlsbad are different, however, because they are surrounded by desert.

Over 250 million years ago, the Carlsbad area was covered with a shallow sea. By the shore of the sea was a **reef**. Plants and sea animals, such as coral, sponges, snails, and clams, lived on this sea shelf. When the plants and animals died, their remains built the reef higher and higher. These remains hardened and turned into limestone. Limestone is a soft rock that is easily changed by elements of nature.

The sea eventually dried up and uncovered the buried reef. The area filled with different particles, such as sand or soil, brought in by wind. These particles are called *sediments*.

Deep beneath these sediments, oil and gases were forming underground. One of these gases was hydrogen sulfide. This is a poisonous gas that smells like rotten eggs.

When rainwater drained down through the rock of Carlsbad, the oxygen in the water mixed with the hydrogen sulfide. This made sulfuric acid.

As time went by, the earth shifted. It pushed and squeezed the limestone. This made big cracks. The sulfuric acid ran into these cracks, making them bigger and bigger. Over time, the acid dissolved and reshaped the limestone. Passageways and large underground chambers were formed.

When the liquid sulfuric acid dissolved limestone, a mineral called *gypsum* was created. Gypsum settled on the floor of these chambers and formed thick piles like underwater snowbanks.

Long after the sulfuric acid drained from the cave, rainwater began to dissolve the limestone. This water carried dissolved limestone into the cave. When the water evaporated, it left behind small amounts of calcite.

Soda straws are dry on the outside because the water runs inside only. This keeps them thin because no calcite builds up on the outside.

This calcite created many of the beautiful formations found in caves. Thin soda straws turned into stalactites. Stalagmites grew up from the cave floor. In time, stalactites and stalagmites met one another and became columns. Draperies hung from the cave's ceilings. The cave walls were decorated with popcorn and flowstone.

All of these cave formations took thousands of years to develop—and the caves will continue to change as water keeps dripping, leaving behind new calcite deposits.

Because of the large amount of hydrogen sulfide in the Carlsbad area, more than 300 caves exist in the Guadalupe Mountains. More than 85 of these caves are located in Carlsbad Caverns National Park.

Popcorn is also called *cave coral* because it resembles the coral limestone formations found in seas and oceans.

Please Don't Touch

Unfortunately, humans also affect the formations in a cave. Just by touching a stalagmite, a piece of flowstone, or a wall of popcorn, people erase the cave's natural beauty. Formations are easily broken, and the oil from human skin can discolor the rock or stop a formation's growth.

CHAPTER 3

Carlsbad Caverns—
Discovered!

Early Cave Dwellers

Native Americans roamed and lived near Carlsbad Caverns as long as 12,000 years ago. They used the limestone cliffs as summer homes.

There is no evidence of Native American life deep within the caverns. But there are signs that early Native Americans used the mouths of caves as protection from weather and enemies. These early cave dwellers drew **pictographs** on the walls of cave entrances.

Jim White

Thousands of years later, a cowboy saw a black swarm of bats coming out of a cavern. His curiosity led him to the huge natural entrance of Carlsbad Cavern.

Standing at the cave's entrance, White peered down into the dark hole. When he couldn't see the bottom, he came up with an idea. He piled some dead cacti and started them on fire. Carefully, he threw one of the burning cacti into the mouth of the cave. It dropped down, down, down until it stopped. The cactus glowed far below the surface of the earth.

But that did not satisfy White's curiosity. He wanted to explore the depths of the dark cave.

Jim White returned to his camp. The camp was filled with cowboys who were building a fence in the area. White made plans to explore the cave. A few days later, he gathered a kerosene lamp, rope, wire, and an ax. He hiked up to the cave in the afternoon. He didn't tell anyone where he'd gone.

The sun slanted into the entrance. White peered in. He thought he could see the bottom. He built a long ladder with the rope and wire. He cut nearby

Rope ladder descending into the cave

Cave formations in the Big Room

shrubs to make the ladder steps and flung his long ladder over the ledge. Starting down the steps, White descended deeper and deeper into the cave. Complete darkness surrounded him.

Suddenly, White reached the end of his ladder. Feeling solid ground beneath him, he stepped off the ladder. Lighting his lamp, he saw he was standing on a ledge. Below him was a narrow tunnel.

White decided to climb down the wall to the tunnel.

It was too dark to see into the tunnel, but White decided to enter it anyway. His little lantern gave off a slight glow as he cautiously made his way through the tunnel. Finally he reached a huge cavern.

Enormous stalactites and stalagmites caught his attention first. He was amazed at the beauty of the cave's formations. White didn't know it, but he was the first person to see the treasures hidden deep inside the cave.

All of a sudden, White's lantern ran out of kerosene. It flickered and went out. He was in complete darkness! Luckily, he was able to find his way back to the wall where his ladder was hanging. White climbed up quickly. He was happy to be back on the surface again. However, he knew he would return to the cave.

When Jim got back to camp, he told the other cowboys what he'd found. No one believed him. He tried to get someone to go down in the cave with him. But no one volunteered.

Jim told many about the beauty and wonder of the cave. Not many people listened though. For many years, White continued to explore the cavern on his own.

Eventually, Ray V. Davis accompanied White on a cave trip and took pictures. These photos were displayed in the town of Carlsbad in 1915. Suddenly people became interested in the cave, and White began to give tours. Finally he was able to share the cavern's wonders with the world!

Believe It or Not!

In 1924, Jim White took a group from *National Geographic* into Carlsbad Cavern. The publicity afterward led reporter Robert Ripley to broadcast a radio report on the cave. Ripley's "Believe It or Not" story made the cavern even more famous.

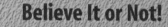

Tiny soda straws make up Doll's Theatre in the Big Room.

CHAPTER 4

Mining
Bat Guano

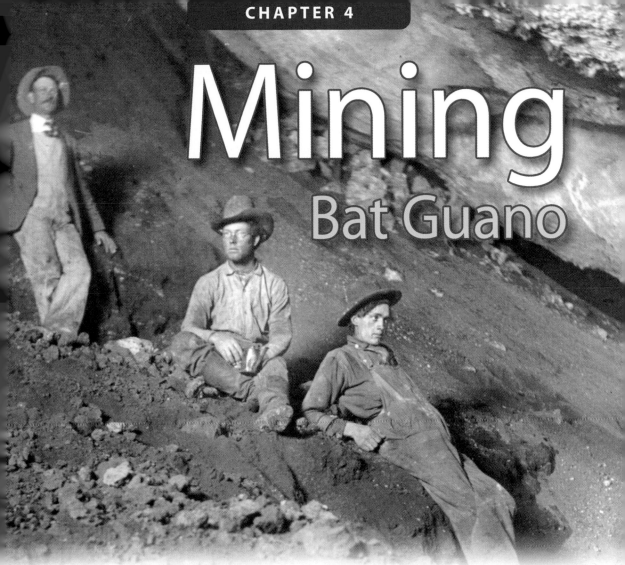

The bats of Carlsbad Cavern did more than just lead Jim White to the cave. These bats became the focus of the cave for 20 years. While people weren't interested in White's stories of the cave's natural wonders, they *were* interested in mining the valuable bat guano found in the cave.

Bat guano, or bat droppings, is an excellent fertilizer. It is used to help plants grow. At the time of Jim White's discovery, tons of bat guano were being used in California to grow oranges.

In some places, the guano in Carlsbad Cavern was layered up to 100 feet. This caught the attention of many miners in the area.

Two shafts were blasted into the bat cave in the early 1900s. Men were hired to mine the guano. They entered and exited the cave in a bucket hooked to a cable. The cable was attached to a gasoline engine, which slowly pulled the cable up and down. The men dropped 170 feet into the dark bat cave. They dug tunnels through the towering guano and stuffed it into **gunnysacks**. Then they dragged the guano up to the surface using iron buckets.

Sometimes the guano miners would take a break and explore the cave. They climbed on top of stalagmites to take pictures. Of course, you can't do this today. If everyone sat on the stalagmites, they would soon be destroyed.

In 20 years, 100,000 tons of guano were mined from Carlsbad Caverns. This valuable mining industry came to an end in 1923 when the caverns were declared a national monument.

Guano Risks

Being around bat guano all the time can lead to a disease called *hystoplasmosis*. Unfortunately, the early miners didn't know about this disease, but many suffered from its effects. Hystoplasmosis affects the lungs and brain and causes a bad cough.

Today when cave explorers enter a cave containing guano, they use breathing masks called *respirators*.

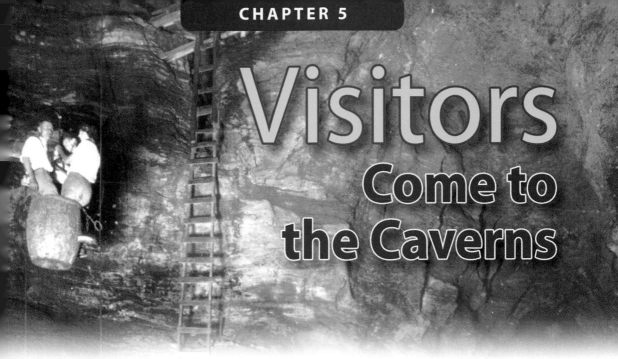

CHAPTER 5

Visitors Come to the Caverns

Early Visitors

When Carlsbad became a national monument, Jim White became its first ranger. From 1923 to 1929, he guided visitors through the Carlsbad Cave National Monument. At the same time, he worked to make the cave more accessible to the public.

At first, just getting to the cave could be quite a challenge. The dirt road was made of loose sand, and cars often got stuck. Many times, passengers had to get out of their cars and push them up the hill to a more solid spot.

The first visitors were lowered into the cave by the old guano-mining bucket. Two people were lowered at a time. When more and more people came to see the cave, this method took too long. A new way to take visitors into the cave became necessary.

These early visitors to the cave include Amelia Earhart, the first woman to fly solo across the Atlantic Ocean.
(Jim White, Amelia Earhart, E. M. Marks, E. H. Marks, and Colonel Tom Boles)

Modern Visitors

Today, tourists visiting Carlsbad Caverns National Park have many ways to explore the area. From the Natural Entrance, a switchback trail takes visitors down to the depths of Carlsbad Cavern. If they're not up to the hike, they can take the elevator, which plunges 750 feet below the earth's surface in less than a minute.

In 1925, Jim White supervised the building of a long wooden staircase into the cave. After the staircase was built, more and more tourists came to see the wonders of Carlsbad. Visitors climbed down the wooden stairs to the bottom of the cave. The path was not lit until 1926. Until then, visitors had to carry their own kerosene lamps to find their way. After their day of exploring, the tourists climbed the steep staircase to the surface.

In 1930, the National Park Service blasted a switchback trail from the natural entrance to the bottom of the cave. The wooden stairs were no longer necessary, so they were removed.

Carlsbad Cavern now has well-lit sidewalks throughout. Signs are posted in front of each site, providing information for visitors. Most of the cavern is open to tourists who want to explore on their own.

However, parts of the cave such as the King's Palace, Queen's Chamber, Green Lake Room, and Papoose Room must be seen with a guided ranger group.

At the bottom of the cave are restrooms, a gift shop, and a small restaurant. Imagine eating lunch 750 feet below the earth! Of course, visitors can also shop and eat above ground.

When walking through Carlsbad, visitors may notice that the temperature is the same throughout the cave. It maintains an average temperature of 56° F. In the summer when outdoor temperatures are in the 90s, the cave is a cool break for tourists. During the winter, rangers sometimes warm up inside the comfortable cave.

Carlsbad Caverns is open year-round. The most popular months for tourism are June, July, and August. However, tourists can visit the cave every day of the year, except Christmas.

Natural Entrance

Safe Spelunking

To explore caves in the Carlsbad area that aren't fully developed for tourists, follow these rules.

- Never go alone. Take at least two other people.

- Tell someone where you're going and when you should be back.

- Carry at least three sources of light, including a waterproof pack of matches and a candle.

- If you do run out of light, stay where you are and wait for someone to find you.

- Wear heavy clothing, boots, knee pads, and a hard hat or helmet.

- Take water, a compass, blanket, first aid kit, watch, and tools for recording your path and findings.

- Leave the cave as you found it. Do not collect souvenirs or touch cave formations.

CHAPTER 6

Creatures
in Carlsbad

The Chihuahuan Desert is home to many interesting creatures. Take a look at some of the unique animals that live in the Carlsbad Caverns National Park.

Mexican Freetail Bats

There are several species of bats at Carlsbad, but the most common is the Mexican freetail bat. The Mexican freetail bat has roosted in Carlsbad for over 5,000 years. About one million of these bats live in the caverns from early spring through October. They **migrate** to Mexico for the winter.

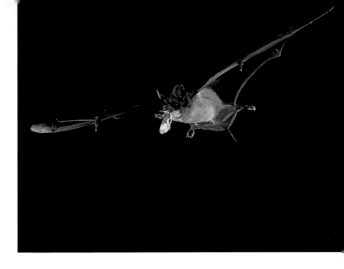

Adopt a Bat

For a small amount of money, you can adopt a bat at Carlsbad. When you adopt a bat, you pledge to protect bats and educate others about them.

These bats arrive in Carlsbad in April to give birth and raise their young. In June, the females have their babies. Usually bats have just one baby. The mother has the baby while hanging from the cave's ceiling by her toes and thumbs. The newborn then clings to the ceiling or its mother.

For the next 4 or 5 weeks, the babies stay with their mothers in the cave. At night, the mothers go out in search of food while the babies stay in the cave. At about 6 weeks, the young bats take their first flight. From then on, they go with their mothers on the nightly search for food. Bats feast on moths and other insects.

One hour before they fly, scouting bats go out to check the light and temperature. The bats remaining in the cave begin to circle. Soon they emerge from the cavern like a black tornado.

Because there are so many bats trying to get out, they sometimes bump into one another and get injured. Ringtail cats and raccoons may enter the cave to look for injured bats to eat.

Staying behind in the cave isn't always guaranteed safety for the baby bats. If a young bat falls from the roost, beetles and cave crickets eat it. These insects live and feed on the bat guano beneath the bat roost.

Scientists at Carlsbad are careful not to disturb the bats in their roost. If they're disturbed, the bats might abandon the cave. To avoid this problem, the scientists use special bat detectors. These detectors show when the bats are flying by displaying echo patterns on a computer screen. Each bat species uses different echo sounds. These sounds tell scientists which species are flying at any given time.

Blind as a Bat

Bats have a different way of "seeing" things. They use echolocation to find their way when flying and to locate prey. Echolocation is the **sonar** system that bats use to "see." The bats send out high frequency sounds that travel through the air. When one of these signals hits an object, it is reflected back and heard by the bat. The bat can then avoid that object or zero in on it.

Cave Swallows

Cave swallows are black birds with pale orange rumps and throats. Their tails have a square tip. Swallows don't sing like some birds, instead they titter.

Cave swallows build their nests in the caves of Carlsbad. This means they share space with the Mexican freetail bats. The cave swallows may be seen circling the cave entrance just before dusk. They know they must hurry to get to their nests before the bats come out. If they don't make it in time, they'll be stuck outside the cave until the bats swarm out.

Usually cave swallows nest in a cave's twilight zone. The twilight zone is the area in a cave that gets direct or indirect light from the entrance. Because of the human-made lights in Carlsbad Cavern, the swallows have nested farther back than they normally would.

Cave swallows are found in caves and sugarcane fields. New Mexico is the farthest north they travel in the United States. They migrate to Carlsbad to nest and have babies.

In 1966, the first cave swallows made their nests in Carlsbad. About 3,000 swallows now call the cave their home.

Western Diamondback Rattlesnakes

A Western diamondback is usually heard before it is seen. When a Western diamondback feels threatened, it flattens its body and coils into an S shape. The tip of its tail rises and rattles. This sound warns other animals or people that the snake is about to strike.

The diamondback will also chase intruders. After it has caught up with its **prey** or enemy, the snake lunges several times to bite. The diamondback's venom is injected into its victim through the snake's fangs. Then the snake swallows its wounded catch. Humans bitten by diamondbacks can become very ill.

Diamondbacks give birth to live young. Once a diamondback is born, it must fight for its life. It may be trampled by the hooves of a deer or cow. Or it may die from extreme heat or cold. Very few young diamondbacks live through their first year.

Badgers have wide bodies that are about 2 feet long. They waddle on their short, strong legs. These animals get their name from the black and white "badges" or markings on their flat heads.

Badgers have very sharp teeth and are excellent fighters. They use their strong front claws to dig out mice, gophers, and other small

Badgers

Badgers usually emerge from their holes about one hour after sunset. These animals hunt at night and sleep during the day. They dig out and live in underground burrows called *setts*. Often badgers pile dirt and stone around their sett's entrance. They are also very clean animals—they change the bedding in their setts often and dig "outhouses" far away from their burrows.

animals for food. One of their favorite foods is earthworms.

When a badger is threatened, it will usually run and hide. If cornered, however, a badger will fight back ferociously.

Cougars

The cougar is also known as the puma or mountain lion. It is the largest cat in North America. This cat looks like a small lioness with short, yellowish brown fur. Cougars can reach up to 8 feet long and weigh 250 pounds. They can leap up to 15 feet in the air and jump down from a 60-foot perch.

The cougar's main food source is deer. It also eats elk, bighorn sheep, and smaller mammals. After the cougar makes a kill, it may sling its prey over its back and carry it away.

Most people working at or visiting Carlsbad Caverns have never seen these large cats. Cougars hunt at night. When they do hunt, they stay hidden while stalking their prey. These animals also avoid humans and rarely attack them.

Roadrunners

Some visitors to the caverns may be greeted by a bird racing down the road, often darting in front of cars and then disappearing into the brush. It's easy to see how the roadrunner got its name.

A roadrunner can sprint at a rate of 15 miles per hour or more. At this speed, the bird's feet barely touch the ground. It uses its wings and long tail to keep its balance. The roadrunner rarely flies.

The roadrunner races to escape danger and catch prey. These birds eat grasshoppers, spiders, scorpions, small birds, lizards, and snakes. To kill larger prey, the roadrunner stabs it with its pointed beak and pounds it on the ground. Then the roadrunner eats it whole.

Turkey Vultures

Another bird of Carlsbad is the turkey vulture. This bird can be seen circling high in the sky. It is an excellent flyer. Turkey vultures glide for long distances without having to beat their wings. They roost in trees and wait for the ground to warm. The rising warm air currents help them take off into the blue sky. If it is raining, turkey vultures stay in the trees all day.

Turkey vultures have sharp eyesight and a strong sense of smell. When flying overhead, these birds can easily spot carrion, or dead animals, miles below. The longer the animal has been dead, the better. Turkey vultures have small beaks. If an animal has been dead for a longer period of time, it is easier for the vulture to tear the meat and eat it. Roadkill is a main food source for the turkey vulture.

Bird of Many Names

The turkey vulture is also called the *buzzard* or the *turkey buzzard*.

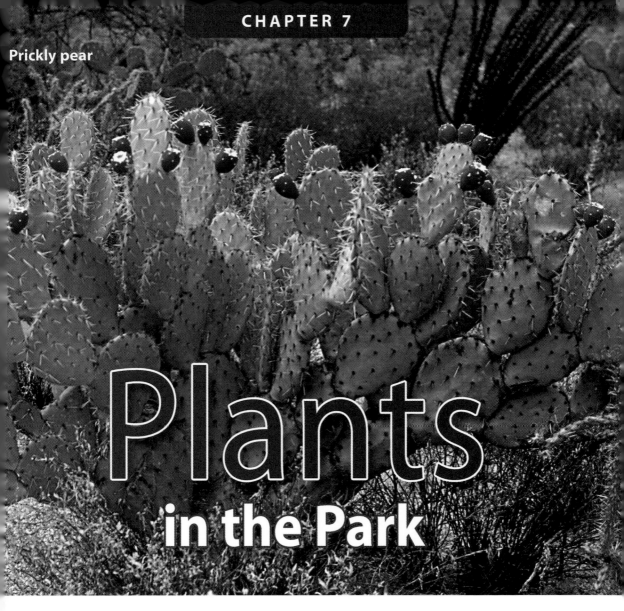

CHAPTER 7

Prickly pear

Plants
in the Park

The Chihuahuan Desert has many beautiful desert plants. These plants have special **adaptations** for survival in the dry, hot climate. The prickly pear, yucca, ocotillo, and lechuguilla are four common plants found in the Carlsbad Caverns area.

Prickly Pear

The prickly pear is a cactus with prickly fruits shaped like pears. The stem of the plant is a series of flat, leaflike sections called *joints*. During the early summer months, large yellow flowers bloom on the edges of the joints.

In the late summer, the joints are covered with red fruits called *tunas*. These fruits are the size of plums and are filled with a red juice.

Pack rats and ground squirrels feed on the prickly pear's spiky pads and tunas. They also dig burrows at the bottom of the plant. They sometimes use the cactus's flat pads to make their nests stronger.

Prickly pears can survive for long periods of time with little water. They do, however, grow better in areas that receive regular rainfall.

Yucca

The yucca is a tall **evergreen** shrub with long, spiky leaves. The yucca's narrow leaves are pointed and stiff. They grow along a stem or in bunches at the end of a stem. White, whitish green, or cream-colored flowers grow in clusters on a stem that pops up from the center of the leaves. These flowers open at night, and some give off a strong fragrance. Yuccas have large fruits that contain many small, flat, black seeds.

Yucca

Yucca Uses

Early Native Americans used the yucca plant for many things. The leaves made strong threadlike material. This was used to make rope, mats, baskets, and sandals. The yucca's flowers and fruit were used for food. The roots of the plant were smashed and made into medicine or soap.

Name That Plant

The ocotillo plant has many names—
candlewood, coachwhip, and vine cactus.
Can you see why?

Ocotillo

The ocotillo is a desert shrub that stands 6 to 25 feet tall. This plant looks like a bunch of dry, spiny sticks growing out of the ground. During most of the year, the dry stems look dead. But after a good rain, green leaves sprout out of the plant's stalk. In April, the ocotillo blossoms with orange-red flowers.

Lechuguilla

The lechuguilla cactus is only found in the Chihuahuan Desert. This plant grows on the rocky limestone slopes found in the Carlsbad Caverns area. By storing water in its thick leaves, the cactus can survive long dry periods.

The lechuguilla has stiff leaves with sharp needles on the tips. These sharp tips can injure the legs of people or animals that brush against them.

Although the lechuguilla plant is small, it produces a large flowering stalk. This takes many years though. The plant has to store up **nutrients** for a long time before it can make the stalk. The flowering stalk grows 6 to 15 feet tall. Once the lechuguilla flowers and produces seeds, the plant dies. Luckily, it has left behind seeds that will grow into new lechuguilla plants.

Lechuguilla

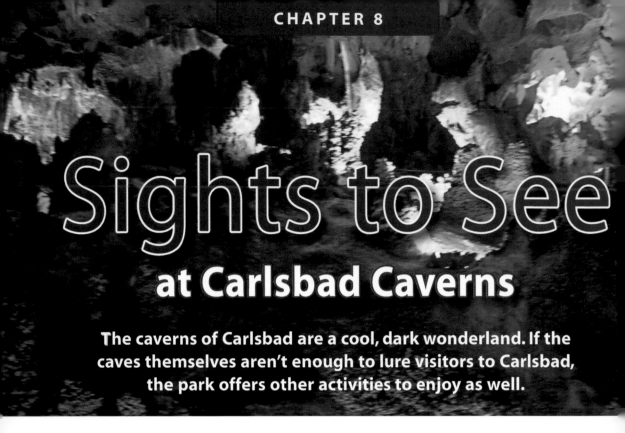

CHAPTER 8

Sights to See

at Carlsbad Caverns

The caverns of Carlsbad are a cool, dark wonderland. If the caves themselves aren't enough to lure visitors to Carlsbad, the park offers other activities to enjoy as well.

Big Room

The Big Room is the largest room in Carlsbad Cavern. The room is 1800 feet long and 250 feet wide. It is filled with huge, beautiful formations.

Many stalagmites decorate the Big Room. The Hall of Giants is a group of huge stalagmites—one of them is almost 60 feet high. The Totem Pole is a tall, slender stalagmite that looks like a totem pole. The oldest of these great stalagmite formations is the Giant Dome. Next to the Giant Dome is Fairyland. This is a large group of stalagmites that look like miniature buildings. So tall that it touches the ceiling, Rock of Ages glistens with many colors.

Familiar Formation

The Lion's Tail in the Big Room is good example of popcorn, or cave coral.

The Bottomless Pit is also located in the Big Room. This is a large hole that was never completely explored until the 1930s. The early explorers of Carlsbad couldn't see the bottom of the pit and thought it was bottomless. Today, the bottom can be seen by shining a strong flashlight into the hole.

How Did They Get Those Names?

Jim White named most of the cave formations in the Big Room.

The Big Room also became the home of the underground lunchroom in 1928. And in January 1932, the first elevator started operating on the edge of the room.

King's Palace Tour

The King's Palace Tour consists of four "decorated" chambers in the deepest portion of the cave, 830 feet beneath the surface. The Palace has a dazzling display of cave formations, including draperies, columns, and soda straws. A ranger-led tour is available for those who wish to enter this royal area of the cavern.

The Green Lake Room is filled with jagged stalactites and rounded stalagmites. A small green pond covers a space on the ground. Entering the room, visitors will find Bashful Baby Elephant. This formation is a stalagmite that looks like a baby elephant with its back turned.

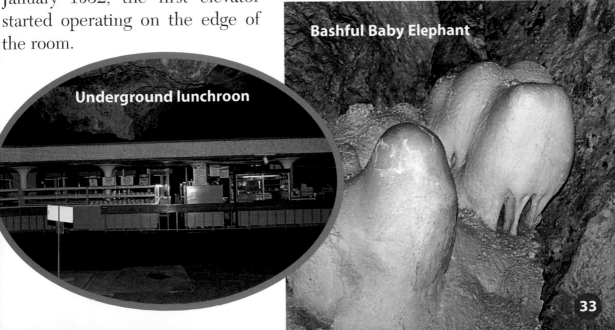

Underground lunchroon

Bashful Baby Elephant

After the Green Lake Room is the King's Palace. It's the deepest room in the cave that visitors can walk through. The palace has a king's bed with stalagmites in the shape of blankets. The Bell Cord is a very thin stalactite about 7 feet 7 inches long and still growing.

Another decorated room is the Queen's Chamber. Near it is Frustrated Lovers. This formation is a stalagmite and a stalactite that almost touch.

During the King's Palace Tour, the ranger may turn off all the lights in the cavern to show the cave's natural darkness. Tourists can imagine themselves as Jim White when his lantern went out!

Frustrated Lovers

The Papoose Room is the fourth decorated cave chamber along the King's Palace Tour.

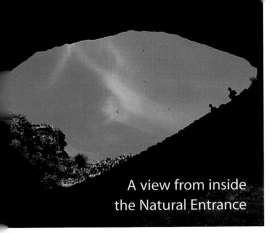

A view from inside the Natural Entrance

Slaughter Canyon Cave

Visitors willing to hike a rough half-mile trail to Slaughter Canyon Cave won't be disappointed. Slaughter Canyon is a wild cave without electricity or paved walkways. Tours of this cave are led by rangers who guide visitors with lanterns and flashlights.

Several special natural formations highlight the tour. At 89 feet, the Monarch is one of the world's tallest columns. A crystal-decorated Christmas Tree column spreads holiday cheer all year long. The Chinese Wall is a fragile dam a few inches high. The cave also contains the remains of old bat guano mining sites.

Natural Entrance

For visitors in good physical condition, the Natural Entrance is the best way to see Carlsbad Cavern. The rough switchback trail winds down deeper and deeper into the black cave. Hikers who make this 750-foot descent will be rewarded by the cavern's attractions.

Baby Hippo is a stalagmite that looks like a baby hippo lying in mud. Beyond Baby Hippo is the Witches Finger. This is a tall, skinny stalagmite that looks like a crooked pointed finger. The Boneyard is a maze of highly dissolved limestone that looks somewhat like Swiss cheese.

At the bottom of the Natural Entrance trail lies Iceberg Rock. Thousands of years ago, this 200,000-ton boulder crashed to the cave floor.

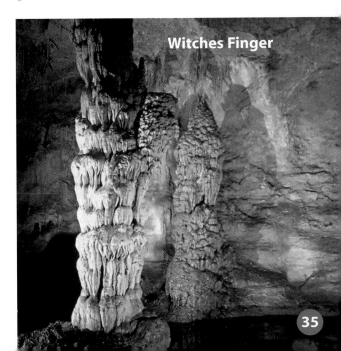

Witches Finger

Take a Hike!

Want to get some fresh air after a long day in the caves? Then take a hike along the 1-mile nature trail. This path begins near the entrance to Carlsbad Cavern and takes you on a nature walk that features desert plants.

The Bats

A very popular evening activity at Carlsbad is bat watching. At dusk from mid-May through the end of September, a ranger speaks at the **amphitheater** in front of the cave mouth. The ranger tells the audience about bats and their habits. In the background, the cave swallows are starting to settle into their nests.

Finally, the Mexican freetail bats swarm out. The dark spiraling of bats exiting the cave can last anywhere from 20 minutes to 2½ hours.

The swarm is the thickest in July and August. This is because the baby bats are now old enough to join their parents in the nightly flight.

Don't Worry

Sometimes one of the bats leaving the cave will fly over the audience's heads. Contrary to popular belief, bats don't fly into people's hair—unless perhaps there are bugs in it!

Tourists await the nightly bat flight.

As the sun sets, bats emerge from the cave.

Carlsbad Caverns Wilderness Area

Tourists wishing to get a good look the Chihuahuan Desert can spend time in the 33,000-acre wilderness area. Many rough trails wind through the desert, providing an up close look at the plants and wildlife. Visitors who walk these trails after a rainstorm will enjoy a beautiful display of desert flowers. At higher elevations, pine woodlands greet hikers.

Walnut Canyon Tour

If you're tired of walking through caves, take a break and hop in your car. The Walnut Canyon Tour is a self-guided scenic drive through the desert. This 9 1/2-mile tour will take you along the Guadalupe Ridge and into upper Walnut Canyon.

Rattlesnake Springs

This natural **spring** has been Carlsbad's main source of water since the 1930s. The spring's streams and **wetlands** provide water and habitats for a variety of mammals, reptiles, and butterflies. Migrating birds often stop at the springs as well.

Shade trees, a picnic area, and restrooms make this area a great stop for lunch or dinner.

Exploring the wonders of Carlsbad Caverns is an exciting experience. Far below the surface of the earth is a magical land created over millions of years. Drop by drop, water decorated the caverns.

All of these wonders were hidden from view until Jim White's curiosity got the best of him. Now the magnificent Carlsbad Cavern is open for all to see. So grab your flashlight, join the bats, and become a spelunker. Carlsbad Caverns awaits your visit.

Carlsbad Caverns Online

To visit Carlsbad Caverns online or get more information about the area, go to the following Web sites.

http://www.nps.gov/cave/index.htm

http://www.nps.gov/cave/teacher guide/fs.history.htm

www.carlsbad.caverns.national-park.com

Glossary

adaptation
characteristic that helps an animal survive in its environment

amphitheater
oval or circular rows of seats arranged around an open space

deposit
matter left behind from a natural process; an accumulation or amount of a material

evaporate
to change from a liquid to a gas

evergreen
having leaves or needles that remain green through all the seasons

gunnysack
bag made of a coarse, heavy fabric like burlap

migrate
to move from one region or climate to another for feeding or breeding

nutrient
material needed by living things for growth

pictograph
drawing or painting on rock walls

prey
animal eaten by another as food

reef
chain of rocks at or near the surface of water

sediments
material deposited by water, wind, or ice

sonar
relating to detecting the location of objects using sound waves

spring
source of water coming from the ground

switchback
zigzagging; having sharp turns back and forth

wetlands
land where the soil contains a lot of moisture

Index